Jesus
the Miracle
Worker

Peter Scothern

New Wine Press

New Wine Press
PO Box 17
Chichester
England PO20 6YB

All Scripture quotations are taken from the Authorised
Version of the Bible. Crown copyright.

ISBN: 1 903725 34 8

Typeset by CRB Associates, Reepham, Norfolk.
Printed in England by Clays Ltd, St Ives plc.

Contents

Chapter 1

Jesus – the Miracle Worker

Compassionate relatives helped cancer stricken Matty Evans into the local market hall. The cruel disease had emaciated her body. She weighed only five stones. For three months she was unable to lie down to prevent her from choking to death; the cancer had lodged in her throat.

The Matty Evans miracle

Matty survived on meagre supplies of soft food and milk. She was very weak and a shadow of her former self. The end was near.

I was moved with compassion when I saw her lying across the front seats. I called the entire assembly to prayer as I stepped down from the platform. A hush came over the assembled company, my prayer was positive with a sense of holy indignation. I felt I must deal with this situation like Jesus in the New Testament. My prayer was authoritative and forthright: **'In the Name of the Lord Jesus Christ I command this cancer to leave this woman's body. Depart now in Jesus' Name and return no more that God may be glorified.'**

A surge of Divine Power

Simultaneously I experienced a tremendous surge of Divine Power like an electric charge. Matty was completely overwhelmed and lay motionless for a while. When she moved she was suddenly alert – she cried out! Her voice was strong and clear. **'I am healed! I am healed!'**

She gave glory to God. We knew something remarkable had occurred.

Matty returned home from that remarkable service in West Wales. She actually requested a supper of fish and chips, but was persuaded to eat something less demanding. She eventually insisted on two slices of toast and a glass of milk. That night she slept perfectly.

The next day she ate a full meal without any trace of discomfort. She made a miraculous recovery. The local hospital later reported no trace of the cancer and Matty Evans enjoyed many years of excellent health.

I have related this remarkable event because I recognise the awesome power God has invested in the Name of His Son Jesus.

The Matty Evans' story is one of many I could relate. Time and time again I have seen the sick and suffering healed through the invincible **Name** of **Jesus**. I have known evil spirits fear and tremble at the mention of His Name.

Miracles in His Name

Recently in Sierra Leone we witnessed the deaf and dumb instantly delivered in the Name of Jesus. We saw God open the eyes of the blind in the Name of Jesus. The media reported these remarkable happenings to the nation.

I will never forget one of my first encounters with evil spirits from the underworld. The event proved so dramatic and unexpected. I was asked to counsel a distressed and demented woman. As I entered the room she immediately went into a rage, swearing and cursing. I tried to calm and console her, thinking this would take the heat out of the situation. She would have none of it!

When demons tremble

On the contrary she became more agitated, aggressive and disturbed, so I resorted to prayer, hoping this would deal with the state of affairs, but when I mentioned the Name of Jesus she reacted violently, shaking and trembling.

Suddenly a deep-throated voice cried out,

'We hate the Name of Jesus.'

'We hate Jesus Christ.'

'We hate Him, we hate Him.'

I was completely taken by surprise, but the most surprising aspect of the affair was the use of the plural 'we' – 'we hate the Name of Jesus'. It was obvious there was more than one evil spirit possessing the woman. I was further shocked by the repeated blaspheming of the Name of Jesus. Finally I got to grips with the situation, binding the evil spirits in the Name of Jesus, I commanded them to depart. She shook and trembled as the evil spirits left her with a chilling cry. For a brief while she lay motionless, then slowly recuperated. Upon realising the wonder of her deliverance she stood upright rendering praise and glory to the Name of Jesus, the very Name she had formerly cursed and blasphemed.

This unforgettable event certainly opened my understanding to the workings of evil spirits and also the awesome Power and Authority invested in the Name of Jesus.

The gospel writers also set on record how the demons testified of the genuine status of Jesus.

This powerful Name

During Christ's early ministry He visited the country of the Gergesenes. Two wild, fierce men emerged from the tombs. They were demon possessed. When Jesus approached them *'they cried out, saying, "What have we to do with thee, Jesus, thou Son of God? art thou come hither to torment us before the time?"'* (Matthew 8:29).

Take careful note of the title 'Son of God', endorsed by the demons. Notice also the demons were aware of their future judgment by Jesus. It is also apparent that more than one demon possessed them. Similar incidents are recorded in the New Testament where the evil spirits confirmed that Jesus was *'the Holy One of God'*, and *'Jesus, thou Son of God'*.

> *'Saying, Let us alone; what have we to do with thee, thou Jesus of Nazareth? art thou come to destroy us? I know thee who thou art, the Holy One of God.'* (Mark 1:24)

'Saying, Let us alone; what have we to do with thee, thou Jesus of Nazareth? art thou come to destroy us? I know thee who thou art; the Holy One of God.' (Luke 4:34)

'And, behold, they cried out, saying, "What have we to do with thee, Jesus, thou Son of God? art thou come hither to torment us before the time?"' (Matthew 8:29)

So while the religious leaders, the Scribes and Pharisees argued and debated concerning the true nature and identity of Jesus, the demons of the underworld gave clear and concise testimony to His true status.

St James also writes:

'Thou believest that there is one God; thou doest well: the devils also believe, and tremble.' (James 2:19)

So there is no doubting the true identity of Jesus as declared by the underworld demons.

God's warning

Reader, God will hold responsible all who cast

doubt upon the true status of His Son Jesus. Jesus declared:

> *'... if ye believe not that I am he, ye shall die in your sins.'* (John 8:24)

A genuine believer will gladly confess,

'Jesus is truly the Son of God.'

Chapter 2

Jesus – the Name and Origin

Jesus: a name adored, a name despised, a name exalted, a name debased, a name cherished, a name blasphemed. No other name has courted so much controversy or caused so much debate.

The Name sent from Heaven

According to inspired records the name 'Jesus' was carried from Heaven on the lips of the arch-angel Gabriel.

Addressing a young virgin, Mary, in the town of Nazareth, Gabriel declared, 'Do not be afraid Mary. You have found favour with God. Listen, you will become pregnant and will give birth to a Son, and you shall call His name Jesus' (Luke 1:30–31). Gabriel further predicted,

> *'The Holy Ghost shall come upon thee, and the*
> *power of the Highest shall overshadow thee ...*
> *that holy thing which shall be born of thee shall*
> *be called the Son of God.'*   (Luke 1:35)

Consequently the virgin Mary seeded her child through an operation of the Holy Spirit. Jesus was directly conceived from the Lord God of Heaven.

The Holy Spirit Himself planted the Divine seed of Jesus in the womb of the virgin. Historical records irrefutably prove that the virgin Mary gave birth to a son and that she called His name Jesus. Unbelievers may reject this testimony but there is indisputable documentary evidence to confirm it.

Remarkable predictions

Meanwhile let us consider the many remarkable predictions by renowned prophets concerning the promised birth of Jesus.

Even the Lord God Himself, at the judgment of the serpent (satan) for his part in the Garden of Eden conspiracy, declared,

> *'And I will put enmity between thee* [satan] *and*
> *the woman* [Eve]*, and between thy seed and her*

14

> *seed; it shall bruise thy head, and thou shalt*
> *bruise his heel.'*　　　　　　　　(Genesis 3:15)

From that hour satan declared all-out war against the seed of the woman. He tried by every devious means to contaminate and destroy her seed.

The first consequence of this evil conspiracy occurred when Cain slew his brother Abel. **Abel was the firstborn seed of the woman Eve**. Throughout history satan has instigated numerous offensives against the seed of the woman.

The Nephilim events preceding the flood judgment in Noah's day, the genocide of the male Hebrew children in the slave camps of Egypt and the murder of the infant innocents during the days of king Herod are confirmed examples.

The Promised Seed

The promised *'Seed of the woman'* eventually destined to bruise satan's head was undoubtedly Jesus:

> *'But when the fullness of the time was come,*
> *God sent forth his Son, made of a woman, made*
> *under the law.'*　　　　　　　　(Galatians 4:4)

Jesus was also the Promised Seed of Abraham, Isaac and Jacob as ancient genealogies in the first chapter of Matthew prove.

Further more the prophet Micah accurately predicted the very birthplace of Jesus,

> *But thou, Bethlehem Ephratah, though thou be little among the thousands of Judah, yet out of thee shall he come forth unto me that is to be ruler in Israel; whose goings forth have been from of old, from everlasting.'* (Micah 5:2)

Daniel also predicted the time of Jesus' birth,

> *'Know therefore and understand, that from the going forth of the commandment to restore and to build Jerusalem unto the Messiah the Prince shall be seven weeks, and threescore and two weeks: the street shall be built again, and the wall, even in troublous times.'* (Daniel 9:25)

The prophet Isaiah prophesied Jesus would be born of a virgin:

> *'Therefore the Lord himself shall give you a sign; Behold a virgin shall conceive, and bear a son, and shall call his name Immanuel.'*
> (Isaiah 7:14)

Jeremiah predicted the Herodian massacre of the infants at the time of Jesus' birth:

> *'Thus saith the* LORD*; A voice was heard in Ramah, lamentation, and bitter weeping; Rahel weeping for her children refused to be comforted for her children, because they were not.'*
>
> (Jeremiah 31:15)

Isaiah also predicted details of Jesus' ministry in Galilee:

> *'Nevertheless the dimness shall not be such as was in her vexation, when at the first he lightly afflicted the land of Zebulun and the land of Naphtali, and afterward did more grievously afflict her by the way of the sea, beyond Jordan, in Galilee of the nations. The people that walked in darkness have seen a great light: they that dwell in the land of the shadow of death, upon them hath the light shined.*
>
> (Isaiah 9:1–2)

The same renowned prophet added further details:

> *'And the spirit of the* LORD *shall rest upon him, the spirit of wisdom and understanding,*

the spirit of counsel and might, the spirit of
knowledge and of the fear of the LORD.'

(Isaiah 11:2)

More amazing predictions

Zechariah predicted the triumphant entry of
Jesus into Jerusalem on Palm Sunday and also
His betrayal for thirty pieces of silver:

'Rejoice greatly, O daughter of Zion; shout, O
daughter of Jerusalem: behold, thy King cometh
unto thee: he is just, and having salvation;
lowly, and riding upon an ass, and upon a colt
the foal of an ass.'   (Zechariah 9:9)

'And I said unto them, If ye think good, give me
my price; and if not, forbear. So they weighed for
my price thirty pieces of silver.'

(Zechariah 11:12)

The Psalmist accurately foretold His betrayal
and subsequent death by crucifixion:

'They that hate me without a cause are more
than the hairs of mine head: they that would
destroy me, being mine enemies wrongfully, are

mighty: then I restored that which I took not away.' (Psalm 69:4)

'For dogs have compassed me: the assembly of the wicked have inclosed me: they pierced my hands and my feet.' (Psalm 22:16)

'They gave me also gall for my meat; and in my thirst they gave me vinegar to drink.' (Psalm 69:21)

'They part my garments among them, and cast lots upon my vesture.' (Psalm 22:18)

In the same Book of Psalms we find the predicted resurrection and ascension of Jesus:

'For thou wilt not leave my soul in hell; neither wilt thou suffer thine Holy One to see corruption.' (Psalm 16:10)

'Thou hast ascended on high, thou hast led captivity captive: thou hast received gifts for men; yea, for the rebellious also, that the LORD God might dwell among them. (Psalm 68:18)

No other Name

Surely, so many renowned prophets having given numerous accurate predictions must conclusively point to Jesus as the Divine fulfilment of these prophecies.

Genuine students of both the Old and New Testaments ultimately accept the weight of evidence is heavily weighted in Jesus' favour. Who else in mankind's history could comply with so many Divine predictions?

The name 'Jesus' is derived from 'Joshua' – meaning 'Saviour', 'Deliverer' – an excellent tribute to Jesus, described by John the Baptist as, *'the Lamb of God, which taketh away the sin of the world'* (John 1:29).

Throughout the fifty-five years of my worldwide Christian ministry I have personally witnessed the awesome Power and Authority invested in the Name of Jesus.

No other name carries the Divine ability to perform such miracles of grace and healing. Surely this is the ultimate proof that the Name 'Jesus' belongs to a person who must be alive and active today. The Holy Scriptures bear witness to this profound fact:

> *'Jesus Christ the same yesterday, and today, and for ever.'* (Hebrews 13:8)

'Neither is there salvation in any other: for there is none other name under heaven given among men, whereby we must be saved.'

(Acts 4:12)

Chapter 3

Jesus – the Son of God?

The sevenfold witness

Some religions look favourably upon Jesus but with certain reservations. They admit He was a remarkable prophet but will not accept His status as the Son of God.

What proof do we have of Jesus' true identity?

▶ *Number 1*

First we acknowledge the testimony of the arch-angel Gabriel during the interview with the Virgin Mary:

> '*And the angel said unto her, Fear not, Mary: for thou hast found favour with God. And, behold, thou shalt conceive in thy womb, and bring forth a son, and shalt call his name JESUS.*'
>
> (Luke 1:30–31)

'And the angel answered and said unto her, The Holy Ghost shall come upon thee, and the power of the Highest shall overshadow thee: therefore also that holy thing which shall be born of thee shall be called the Son of God.'

(Luke 1:35)

Gabriel is the elected angel of annunciation receiving authority and instruction directly from the Lord God in Heaven.

▶ *Number 2*
Secondly, we have God's personal witness from Heaven:

'And Jesus, when he was baptized, went up straightway out of the water: and, lo, the heavens were opened unto him, and he saw the Spirit of God descending like a dove, and lighting upon him: And lo a voice from heaven, saying, This is my beloved Son, in whom I am well pleased.' (Matthew 3:16–17)

'Now when all the people were baptized, it came to pass, that Jesus also being baptized, and praying, the heaven was opened. And the Holy Ghost descended in a bodily shape like a dove

upon him, and a voice came from heaven, which said, Thou art my beloved Son; in thee I am well pleased.' (Luke 3:21–22)

'And John bare record, saying, I saw the Spirit descending from heaven like a dove, and it abode upon him. And I knew him not: but he that sent me to baptize with water, the same said unto me, Upon whom thou shalt see the Spirit descending, and remaining on him, the same is he which baptizeth with the Holy Ghost. And I saw, and bare record that this is the Son of God.' (John 1:32–34)

▶ *Number 3*

Thirdly, the witness of the Roman centurion and those who attended the crucifixion of Jesus:

'Now when the centurion, and they that were with him, watching Jesus, saw the earthquake, and those things that were done, they feared greatly, saying, Truly this was the Son of God.' (Matthew 27:54)

▶ *Number 4*

Fourthly, the witness of the demons and devils of the underworld:

'And, behold, they cried out saying, What have we to do with thee, Jesus, thou Son of God? art thou come hither to torment us before the time?'
(Matthew 8:29)

'Saying, Let us alone; what have we to do with thee, thou Jesus of Nazareth? art thou come to destroy us? I know thee who thou art, the Holy One of God.'
(Mark 1:24)

'And devils also came out of many, crying out, and saying, Thou art Christ the Son of God. And he rebuking them suffered them not to speak: for they knew that he was Christ.'
(Luke 4:41)

▶ *Number 5*
Fifthly, the witness of notorious Legion of Gadara:

'And when he was come out of the ship, immediately there met him out of the tombs a man with an unclean spirit, who had his dwelling among the tombs; and no man could bind him, no, not with chains: ... But when he saw Jesus afar off, he ran and worshipped him, and cried with a loud voice, and said, What have I to do with thee, Jesus, thou Son of the most high God? I adjure thee by God, that thou torment me not.'
(Mark 5:2–3, 6–7)

▶ *Number 6*

Sixthly, the witness of the Apostle Peter and Christ's confirmation:

> 'When Jesus came into the coasts of Caesarea Philippi, he asked his disciples, saying, Whom do men say that I the Son of man am? And they said, Some say that thou art John the Baptist: some, Elias; and others, Jeremias, or one of the prophets. He saith unto them, But whom say ye that I am? And Simon Peter answered and said, Thou art the Christ, the Son of the living God. And Jesus answered and said unto him, Blessed art thou, Simon Bar-jona: for flesh and blood hath not revealed it unto thee, but my Father which is in Heaven.'
>
> (Matthew 16::13–17)

▶ *Number 7*

Seventhly, satan tempts Jesus but knows Jesus is the Son of God:

> 'And the devil said unto him, If thou be the Son of God, command this stone that it be made bread. And Jesus answered him saying, It is written, That man shall not live by bread alone, but by every word of God.'
>
> (Luke 4:3–4)

Remember once again the challenging words of Jesus:

'I said therefore unto you, that ye shall die in your sins: for if ye believe not that I am he, ye shall die in your sins.' (John 8:24)

Also:

'Thou believest that there is one God; thou doest well: the devils also believe, and tremble.'
(James 2:19)

Chapter 4

Jesus –
Why the Crucifixion?

One of the most intriguing mysteries concerning Jesus must be His crucifixion. How could some-one with formidable power to calm the elements, raise the dead, and cast out devils be finally subjected to the horror of crucifixion? As we closely consider this matter let us clarify one important factor.

Jesus predicted His crucifixion

Jesus made clear and plain well in advance that He was fully aware of the fate that awaited Him. This fact also startled and astounded His disciples. Jesus said:

> *'I am the good shepherd: the good shepherd giveth his life for the sheep.'*
>
> (John 10:11, my emphasis)

'No man taketh it [my life] *from me, but **I lay it down of myself.** I have power to lay it down* [crucifixion], *and I have power to take it again* [resurrection].' (John 10:18, my emphasis)

'*And Jesus going up to Jerusalem took the twelve disciples apart in the way, and said unto them, Behold, we go up to Jerusalem; and the **Son of man shall be betrayed unto the chief priests and unto the scribes**, and they shall **condemn him to death**, and they shall deliver him to the Gentiles to **mock, and to scourge, and to crucify him**: and the third day **he shall rise again**.*' (Matthew 20:17–19, my emphasis)

This prediction was accurately and scrupulously fulfilled.

Jesus knew He was destined to be crucified. He knew well in advance. Even when the disciples remonstrated against the idea Jesus rebuked them. He was absolutely determined to proceed with His destiny. His crucifixion and death were predetermined. They were essential to God's will and purpose.

Why the cross?

But why did Jesus suffer the cross? To completely understand this mystery we must consider some very important divine principles. First, that God recognized mankind's overwhelming problem was the **'sin'** problem.

Let me explain. Human nature is distorted and warped. Interwoven in our natures are evil aspirations as well as good aspirations: for example, we can love but we can hate; we can be loyal but we can be jealous; we can believe but we can doubt; we can be kind but we can be cruel.

The more serious problems arise when evil aspirations overtake our good aspirations: for example, cruelty can turn to murder; selfishness can breed rape and sexual exploitation; jealousy can divide families and cause a myriad problems; lust can lead to drug addiction and similar overwhelming, self-destructive passions. When humans experience such levels of self-inflicted addictions they become ensnared and enslaved. Depression, despair, and despondency are common maladies these days. Sufferers will pay any price to be healed and delivered.

Jesus moves with compassion

Jesus was moved with compassion when confronted with victims of evil and illness. He was totally committed to healing the sick in mind, spirit, and body.

> *'God anointed Jesus of Nazareth with the Holy Ghost and with **power: who went about doing good, and healing all that were oppressed of the devil.'*** (Acts 10:38, my emphasis)

Jesus healed all manner of sickness and disease. But above all **He was able to transform human nature and change human lives**. He completely transformed **Saul of Tarsus** from a destroyer of Christians into a saintly person. He changed money-seeking Matthew into a compassionate apostle. He lifted **Mary Magdalene** out of prostitution into a godly life. Jesus worked miracles of grace by imparting His very own nature into contaminated lives.

The 'born again' experience

The disciples of Jesus were not simply followers but individuals whose lives were completely transformed by His power. This was the **'born again'** experience Jesus refers to in the Gospel of St John:

> *'Jesus answered and said unto him, Verily, verily, I say unto thee, Except a man be born again, he cannot see the kingdom of God.*
> *Nicodemus saith unto him, How can a man be*

*born when he is old? can he enter the second
time into his mother's womb, and be born?*

*Jesus answered, Verily, verily, I say unto thee,
Except a man be born of water and of the Spirit, he
cannot enter into the kingdom of God. That which
is born of the flesh is flesh; and that which is born
of the Spirit is spirit. Marvel not that I said unto
thee, Ye must be born again.'* (John 3:3–7)

The second birth is a life-changing, nature-
transforming experience. Evil ways and habits
evaporate as the indwelling presence of Jesus fills
our lives. However, Jesus' ability to perform these
miracles, while on earth, was limited to His
immediate periphery. Something had to be done
to release this life-transforming power to the
entire human race. And this is why Jesus
submitted to crucifixion. In the inspired words
of the apostle Peter:

*'Who his own self bare our sins in his own body
on the tree* [cross], *that we, being dead to sins,
should live unto righteousness: by whose stripes
ye were healed.'* (1 Peter 2:24)

The heart revelation

This is the heart revelation of the crucifixion.
Jesus submitted Himself to crucifixion in order to

take upon Himself the **sins and ills of mankind**. Jesus died **bearing our sins in His body on the cross**. Such was the trauma that Jesus cried out, *'My God, my God, why has thou forsaken me?'* (Matthew 27:46).

Even the elements witnessed to the crucifixion drama. The sunlight ceased for three hours shrouding the area in darkness. An earthquake struck the locality and the rocks were rent. The veil in the temple was torn asunder. Jesus' final words *'It is finished!'* (John 19:30) rent the air. Notice – **not** 'I am finished' **but** *'It is finished'*. Jesus had triumphantly completed His divine quest to secure salvation and forgiveness for all mankind.

Another amazing facet of this sacrificial act was the shedding of Jesus' blood. The Holy Scriptures state *'without shedding of blood is no remission* [for sin]*'* (Hebrews 9:22). Jesus made certain His death included the shedding of His blood to fulfil the Scriptures. Forgiveness and reconciliation were made available to a fallen human race.

Do you understand?

Reader, Jesus had **you** upon His heart and mind when He submitted to the horrors of crucifixion.

'Greater love hath no man than this, that a man lay down his life for his friends.'

(John 15:13)

'For God so loved the world, that he gave his only begotten Son, that whosoever believeth in him should not perish, but have everlasting life.'

(John 3:16)

My conversion

I remember the evening I was seriously ill and bedridden. My young life seemed to be ebbing away. My faith in God was at its lowest point. Out of sheer desperation tears ran down my cheeks as I called upon the God of heaven. I really meant business with God.

Suddenly the room brightened and I experienced my first vision. The crucifixion scene was re-enacted before me. I can remember the details to this day. The climax came when Jesus looked down from the cross quoting these most blessed words: 'Son, thy sins be forgiven thee.' The peace of God flooded my heart. I knew from that moment God had forgiven me for Christ's sake. I was reborn of the Spirit of God. My life was completely transformed. I knew God was on the inside of my being. I would never be the same again. My conversion occurred some fifty years ago. Jesus is more real today then ever before.

How about you?

Reader, have you experienced God's life-changing grace and power? Do you know the indwelling peace of God which passes all understanding? Have you been 'born again'? Jesus is longing to step out of the Bible and fill your life with His power and presence. If you seek Him with all your heart you will surely find Him. Call upon His Name – **Jesus** – and invite Him into your life.

Chapter 5

Is Jesus Alive?

Nothing is more controversial about Jesus than His resurrection. Did He in reality rise from the dead? Or was this one of history's greatest hoaxes? Did the Jewish Sanhedrin bribe the guardians of the tomb and testify that His body was snatched away by His disciples? Or did the disciples secretly convey Jesus' body to some other location?

The documented evidence

Let us carefully consider the documented evidence. Following the death of Jesus two of His trusted friends were given permission to place His body in the new tomb of His great uncle Joseph of Arimathea. Pontius Pilate the local Roman Governor was acquainted with Joseph and Nicodemus. They were members of the Sanhedrin and could be relied upon to ensure the safety of Jesus' body in the tomb.

To avoid confrontation with the Jewish authorities, Pilate agreed to seal the sepulchre with his personal seal. He also permitted the Jews to appoint their own guardian although overseen by a Roman army officer. Every precaution was taken to ensure no-one tampered with the burial chamber.

The angelic witness

In other words, the only way Jesus could have vacated the sepulchre was by some supernatural means. The documented evidence relates how a great earthquake shook the vicinity of the tomb. The huge stone sealing the entrance was cast aside by a mighty force. The guardians of the tomb were so terrified they fled the scene. No doubt Peter and John were alerted by the disturbance and rushed down to the sepulchre. They found the huge stone rolled away from the entrance.

> 'They entered in [the tomb], *and found not the body of the Lord Jesus … as they were much perplexed thereabout, behold, two men stood by*

them in shining garments: ... they said unto
them, Why seek ye the living among the dead?
He is not here, but is risen: remember what he
*spake unto you ... The Son of man **must** ... be*
crucified, and the third day rise again.'

(Luke 24:3, 4, 5, 7)

The resurrection predicted

The disciples then recollected that Jesus had
predicted the events foretold of His crucifixion
and resurrection. For a further forty days Jesus
appeared alive and well. For almost six weeks *'he*
*shewed himself alive after his passion by **many***
infallible proofs, being seen of them ... and
speaking of things pertaining to the kingdom
of god' (Acts 1:3). 'What infallible proofs?' we
may ask.

Thomas the sceptic convinced

Jesus personally appeared to the most sceptical of
the twelve disciples. His name was Thomas called
Didymus – who emphatically refused to believe
Jesus was risen from the dead. Thomas insisted
on touching **the risen body** to prove for himself
that Jesus was alive.

'And after eight days again his disciples were within, and Thomas with them: then came Jesus, the doors being shut, and stood in the midst, and said, Peace be unto you.

Then saith he to Thomas, Reach hither thy finger, and behold my hands; and reach hither thy hand, and thrust it into my side: and be not faithless, but believing.

And Thomas answered and said unto him, My Lord and my God.

Jesus saith unto him, Thomas, because thou hast seen me, thou hast believed: blessed are they that have not seen, and yet have believed.'

(John 20:26–29)

Also carefully note verses 30 and 31.

Forty days following His resurrection a company of 500 disciples gathered on Mount Olivet to witness the departure of Jesus to heaven. They listened to His final instructions. Many of these were present on the day of Pentecost when the Holy Ghost came upon them with great power and glory.

Five hundred witnesses

For such a large company to come together in one particular location at one particular time must have been divinely planned. Indeed it was!

> 'After that, he was seen of above five hundred brethren at once; of whom the greater part remain unto this present, but some are fallen asleep.'   (1 Corinthians 15:6)

The destroyer Saul of Tarsus also encountered the **risen Jesus**:

> 'For I delivered unto you first of all that which I also received, how that Christ died for our sins according to the scriptures; and that he was buried, and that he rose again the third day according to the scriptures: and that he was seen of Cephas then of the twelve.'
>
>   (1 Corinthians 15:3–5)

> 'After that, he was seen of James; then of all the apostles. And last of all he was seen of me also, as of one born out of due time.'
>
>   (1 Corinthians 15:7–8)

Following Jesus' resurrection and ascension, miracle after miracle was performed by His disciples. These signs occurred as further infallible proof of His resurrection. Only a **living Jesus** could continue to perform such divine wonders. No other person in human history has performed such amazing miracles after their decease. Following His resurrection Jesus had promised **His presence would always accompany His true disciples.**

> *'So then after the Lord had spoken unto them, he was received up into heaven, and sat on the right hand of God. And they went forth, and preached every where, the Lord working with them, and confirming the word with signs following.'*
>
> (Mark 16:19–20)

The sceptics convinced

Even the close disciples of Jesus initially doubted His resurrection. However, Jesus provided all the proof and evidence they requested. The disciples touched Him, conversed with Him, and dined with Him. Finally, He gave them the following instructions:

> *'Afterward he appeared unto the eleven as they sat at meat, and upbraided them with their unbelief and hardness of heart, because they believed not them which had seen him after he was risen.*

And he said unto them, Go ye into all the world, and preach the gospel to every creature. He that believeth and is baptized shall be saved; but he that believeth not shall be damned. And these signs shall follow them that believe; In my name shall they cast out devils; they shall speak with new tongues; they shall take up serpents; and if they drink any deadly thing, it shall not hurt them; they shall lay hands on the sick, and they shall recover.' (Mark 16:14–18)

For two thousand years the genuine followers of Jesus have proclaimed His kingdom message. They have continued to provide divine evidence of His resurrection by healing the sick, casting out evil spirits and working miracles in His all-powerful Name.

My files contain many present-day testimonies of lives radiantly transformed and the sick healed by the risen Jesus. These remarkable signs are infallible proof that Jesus is alive today.

'And with great power gave the apostles witness of the resurrection of the Lord Jesus: and great grace was upon them all.' (Acts 4:33)

'But ye shall receive power, after that the Holy Ghost is come upon you: and ye shall be witnesses

unto me both in Jerusalem, and in all Judea, and in Samaria, and unto the uttermost part of the earth.' (Acts 1:8)

Jesus the same today

The Holy Scriptures declare:

'Jesus Christ the same yesterday, and today, and for ever.' (Hebrews 13:8)

If you believe this divine statement – **Jesus must be alive today**. And not just a **living Jesus** but the **unchanged**, incomparable **Jesus**. In other words **Jesus** is able **to perform His miracles of grace and healing** *today*. Many believe **Jesus** worked wonders in New Testament days but **not today**. Their estimation of Jesus is contrary to God's Word. They are preaching and teaching a Jesus different from the New Testament Jesus. I believe Jesus is **the same today** exactly as stated in the Holy Scriptures. **He is the Saviour of the world, the healer of our diseases and able to do** *'exceeding abundantly above all that we ask or think'* (Ephesians 3:20).

The Bible says Jesus is the same today. So who do we believe? The sceptics, the doubters, or the infallible Word of God?

Chapter 6

Jesus Alive?
Present-Day Witnesses

Throughout the Christian era there have been sceptics who have attempted to disprove and discredit the truth concerning Jesus. However, one thing overshadows their scepticism. Such doubters cannot erase or eradicate the genuine experiences of those who have personally encountered the Living Jesus. Saul of Tarsus is a classic example. I share with you a selection of genuine experiences related by those who have been privileged to meet the Living Jesus.

Witnesses among the children

Christ's compassion and concern for the children is indelibly stamped upon the gospel records. Even when the disciples turned the little ones away Jesus insisted on blessing them. I have always respected the simple uncomplicated faith of a child. I can pray for them with supreme confidence.

During the remarkable Calcutta Crusade I visited the circus grounds to check the preparations. While conversing with a company of local ministers we were suddenly confronted by a distressed father carrying a sick child. The little one had been bitten by a scorpion, and was crying bitterly. Her leg was beginning to swell and I will never forget the look of fear in her dark eyes. Taking the child in my arms, I authoritatively commanded the poison to leave her in the Name of Jesus. The Lord's Power flowed freely into little her body. Immediately the pain disappeared and within seconds she was smiling with gratitude. I handed her back to her father who bowed gratefully and began giving praise to God. The ministers also joined in the celebration glorifying the Name of Jesus.

God's timing is perfect

A distressed mother desperately pushed her way to the front of my crowded service. 'Are you the

Rev. Scothern? My daughter is desperately ill in the local hospital; she has been in a coma for several days in the Intensive Care Unit. Please, please offer a prayer for her tonight.'

I assured her that all would be well. So at precisely ten minutes to eight I invited the congregation to stand and join hands in compassion and faith for the young girl's restoration. The believing prayers from the assembly were so spontaneous that many promptly burst into praise and thanksgiving anticipating a miracle. The service concluded about 9.30 pm.

As the folks were dispersing the mother of the sick child returned to the meeting. Her face was radiant with joy as she pushed to the front. 'Bless God, my daughter is out of her coma. I have been talking to her!' she excitedly proclaimed as she shared the good news with the rest of the congregation.

As an afterthought I publicly enquired of her, 'about what time did your daughter make this miraculous recovery?'

'At about ten minutes to eight!' she replied. An anthem of praise emanated from the congregation. This was precisely the time that believing prayer had been offered for the sick child. Did not Jesus instruct us to believe our prayers were heard the very moment we pray?

A miracle in Liverpool

'She can skip now,' testified the excited father!

I was crusading in the Wellington Road Baptist Church, Dingle, Liverpool, for two unforgettable weeks. Hundreds thronged the place nightly witnessing many dramatic healings, including that of ten-year-old Marion Kerr.

Removing her leg irons her mother watched with tear-filled eyes as Marion walked up and down the church aisle strong and well.

The local press reporters visited the home of the young miracle child and found Marion skipping outside her home. Her photograph and testimony appeared on the front page of the Liverpool Weekly News.

An amazing miracle

Perhaps one of the most amazing miracle healings I have ever witnessed was reported in detail by the BBC in an enthralling documentary entitled *The Kilgetty Healer*. This unique programme was shown on the BBC2 network during August 1975. X-rays were presented on the programme to give indisputable evidence to the reality of the miracle.

'He needs an operation. We'll send for him.'

Before these words could sink in, Mr and Mrs King were ushered briskly out of the specialist's consulting room. Stephen their twenty-month-old son was limping beside them.

It was in June 1970 that the orthopaedic specialist studied Stephen's X-ray. He declared that there was no hip socket on the right side necessitating an early operation. There was no bone where there should have been and there was bone where there should not have been. The hip joint was completely dislocated and one leg was shorter than the other. A major operation was needed. Mr and Mrs King asked for a second opinion and visited an eminent orthopaedic specialist in Birmingham. A further X-ray was taken.

After studying it the specialist said, 'I am sorry I have to agree that Stephen urgently requires an operation on the right hip and there is no other solution. Without it Stephen will be permanently crippled.'

Being a State Registered Nurse, Mrs King knew what the operation would entail. It would mean weeks or maybe months in plaster of paris. Furthermore, she was certain that the hospital-isation of Stephen would cause serious emotional problems, as several enforced separations during babyhood had already affected him. As a mother she was very sad and burdened, but how precious it is during such times to know the friendship of Jesus. Mr and Mrs King simply handed their problem over to the Lord.

The healing revelation

At this point God revealed to Stephen's mother something she had never previously realised. Their Bible reading the following morning centred around the eighth chapter of Matthew. The Holy Spirit illuminated verse seventeen in a new and living way:

> '[Jesus] *Himself took our infirmities and bare our sicknesses.'*

They had previously acknowledged that Jesus had borne their **sins** on the Cross, but now saw clearly that He also bore our **sickness**. They further rejoiced in verse sixteen where it faithfully declares that Jesus healed all that were sick.

Also they claimed the promise *'Jesus Christ the same yesterday and today and for ever'* (Hebrews 13:8).

Mr and Mrs King explained to their specialist how they felt concerning faith in God's Word. He replied, 'Faith is alright in its place, but this is not just a question of healing. Your son needs a complete reconstruction of the hip joint and this can only be accomplished by a surgical operation.'

Faithfully supported by the prayers of Christian friends Stephen's parents held fast to the promises of God. For a while Stephen continued to limp badly and could not walk without falling. Then through a remarkable series of circumstances they were introduced to my God-given ministry. They promptly wrote to me requesting prayer and I mailed a faith-inspired letter along with an anointed prayer cloth (Acts 19:11–12).

That night, while Stephen slept, Mrs King laid the prayer cloth over his right hip, in the Name of Jesus, asking God to work a creative miracle.

Although Stephen was lying perfectly still, Mrs King felt movement in the hip beneath her hand. Within moments God created a new bone and miraculously performed the reconstruction. The following morning Stephen was able to jump, skip, climb and even kick a football. He kept running up and down the fifty-foot-long drive without falling.

During August Stephen's parents returned to visit the orthopaedic specialist and a new X-ray was taken. He studied it very carefully and then compared it with the previous X-rays. He then informed Mr and Mrs King **that both hips** were normal and the pending operation was unnecessary. The final X-ray proved scientifically that God's Power had touched Stephen, making him whole. Stephen later invited Christ into his heart.

All praise and glory to God.

Eczema vanishes in Jesus Name

Billy had suffered with eczema since he was a baby in arms. He was nearly eight years of age when he attended my healing service in South Yorkshire. I distinctly remember Billy rolling up his coat sleeve and saying, 'Can God cure this?'

'Yes Billy, if you trust Him with all your heart and serve Him with all your strength,' I replied.

'That's great,' said Billy and I promptly anointed him with oil in the Name of Jesus.

The following month I returned to the same Baptist Church. Billy was there waiting on the steps of the chapel, his face was beaming with delight.

I was greeted with 'He's done it! He's done it!'

Sure enough Billy's arms were completely clear of eczema. God had removed every trace. Billy gave testimony to a packed and praising congregation that same evening.

Young boy Jason receives healing

I was ministering in a West Wales Baptist Church and the congregation included a company of travelling folk. Young Jason Roberts suffered a serious heart defect. His mother presented him to the Lord when I requested the sick and suffering to come forward.

Jason observed the proceedings with rapt attention and showed no sign of shyness!

Laying my hands upon him in the Lord's Name I distinctly experienced God's Power surging through me. I **knew** Jason was healed. Turning to his mother I said, 'God has healed your son, follow after the Lord and serve Him faithfully.'

Having set Jason down on the floor I instructed him to run up and down the aisle. Without hesitation the young lad raced around the chapel, and returned to the front, showing no sign of his heart complaint. His mother lifted up her hands and gave praise to God. Jason later attended a Cardiff Hospital where he was informed that his heart was sound and normal.

'Jesus miraculously healed my son of a hole in the heart'

(The personal testimony of Mrs Roberts)

'Jason was born in Pembroke, West Wales during 1972. From the very tender age of ten days we discovered that he was suffering from a hole in the heart. He was a very weak and sickly child, always attending hospital. We were very anxious and concerned about his future.

When Jason was two years old we heard that healing Evangelist Peter Scothern was holding a special healing service at the Baptist Church Pembroke. We attended the service taking Jason with us. At the invitation we went forward and brother Peter laid hand upon our little son in the Name of Jesus. God's servant prayed very positively and we put our trust in the Lord.

From that time Jason grew up and began running around, kicking a football and doing everything a normal boy would do. He has never once complained of his heart and has always been healthy and well.

Eight months ago we attended the hospital at Cardiff and subsequent tests have proved a pending operation is not necessary, and that Jason's heart is completely healed.

Every time brother Peter ministers in the area, we take Jason along to testify. Last week, he ran up and down the aisle of the Baptist Church to show the congregation that the Lord had miraculously healed him.'

[*This testimony provided by Jason's parents, Mr and Mrs Roberts, of Pembroke, Dyfed, West Wales.*]

Andrew received supernatural hair

Young Andrew was born without any hair cells in his body. By the time he was eight years old his condition became most embarrassing. Some of Europe's leading specialists confirmed that his problem was incurable.

Returning home from school one day he received a handbill advertising our Divine Healing Services in the village of Summerhill. His grandmother agreed to accompany him. Young Andrew listened intently to the Gospel message and was fully persuaded that Jesus would heal him.

Andrew presented himself for the laying on of hands, and returned home full of expectancy.

Every morning afterwards he would say to his parents, 'Look and see if my hair is growing.' Andrew never once doubted the Lord would heal him. Some eight weeks later he experienced the first signs of new growth on his head.

Slowly but progressively Andrew's hair grew. He thanked God each day for his miracle – exactly as I had instructed him. Eventually the young boy was blessed with normal natural hair.

One evening Andrew again joined the healing line. 'Why have you come for prayer again?' I asked him.

'Uncle Peter,' he replied, 'my hair is growing curly like a little girl's, and I want it to grow straight!'

Believe it or not, God answered this prayer also. Everyone was so excited and gave glory to God.

Totally deaf ears opened

Maria was six years old when I visited Abeokuta, Nigeria for the memorable West African Crusade. The local chief allowed me the use of the palace grounds. I can recall a dozen prisoners hauling large pieces of timber to construct the platform.

There was a tremendous interest in the Crusade. The very first evening some two thousand inhabitants gathered to hear the Gospel and witness the mighty works of God. As I stepped onto the platform someone lifted a child into my arms. It was little Maria, I will never forget her beautiful eyes and rich, dark skin. I enquired as to why I was handed the little girl.

A local man replied in broken English, 'She cannot hear she is deaf.'

The eyes of all present were centred upon the platform. I took Maria in my arms and prayed compassionately for Jesus to heal her for the glory of God. At first nothing happened, so I prayed a second time, commanding Maria's ears to be opened in the Name of Jesus. As soon as I removed my hands her face radiated with assurance. First I clapped my hands quietly and she nodded approval. I repeated the action more loudly and she promptly put her hands over her ears. The noise was too intense, for Maria's deaf ears had miraculously opened. I then proceeded with two-syllable words, 'Ma-ma, Da-da'. Maria spoke her first words.

Suddenly the congregation erupted with shouts of praise. Within seconds a score or more little children were pushed onto the platform to be blessed. So many children needed Divine healing. The following day when I visited Maria at her home to take her details and photographs.

I discovered she was beginning to speak additional words. The entire population attended the Crusade to hear the glorious Gospel of Jesus Christ and to witness God confirming His Word with signs following.

Blind Sierra Leone girl instantly healed

I was crusading for Christ in Freetown, Sierra Leone during 1985. Thousands attended services in the central park.

One evening a young girl, blind in both eyes, suddenly received her sight. She cried out with joy. 'God made me see! God made me see!'

I promptly jumped down from the platform, while the crowd pushed the young girl to the front. Sure enough the young girl could see everything and excitedly pointed in every direction. I lifted her onto the platform for everyone to see as she demonstrated her new sight. A great shout of praise to God resounded through the multitude.

Incredible miracle in the USA

During my first visit to the United States I was introduced to Ronald Coyne. He was blind in one eye, and wore an artificial eye. His testimony was almost unbelievable.

One day Ronald went forward to receive Divine healing. Upon receiving the laying on of hands, he experienced a brilliant light in his blind eye. From that moment Ronald Coyne could see perfectly through his artificial eye.

This phenomena astounded everyone. Even I found it hard to believe, but when I personally tested his sight I was obliged to acknowledge that Ronald Coyne could see perfectly through an 'artificial eye!'

> *'Is **any thing** too hard for the LORD?'*
> (Genesis 18:14, my emphasis)

Making the dumb to speak

During one of my memorable Gospel crusades in Freetown, Sierra Leone, thousands gathered in the central public park. Many sick and afflicted attended those great open-air services. They would arrive hours before the start and sit patiently under large black umbrellas to protect themselves from the burning sun.

One evening after the service commenced a charabang of young children arrived. Their ages ranged from five to twelve years. They all shared a common ailment – they were deaf and dumb. The stewards guided them to the front of the vast congregation. I was directed by the Lord to invite the local clergy, priests and deacons to come forward and stand with the children. Each minister was requested to select a child and lay hands over their ears in the all-powerful Name of Jesus. A holy hush fell upon the congregation. The Lord enabled me to pray with great power and authority.

> 'Lord Jesus, glorify Your Name and show forth Your omnipotent power and boundless compassion – show these people that You are the living Lord, and Creator of all things. Command the opening of every deaf ear and the loosing of every dumb tongue – among these little children for Your praise and glory.'

Suddenly the Holy Spirit descended upon the ministers and the children. Remarkably the first miracle which occurred was the instant healing of a blind ten-year-old. The girl suddenly cried out that she could see the lights and the faces of the folk around her.

This spontaneous Divine happening electrified the proceedings. The ministers quickly discovered that some of the deaf children were beginning to hear clearly and distinctly. There was tremendous excitement as one by one the children were lifted to the platform. Speaking directly into their little ears I would use words like, 'Ma-ma', 'Da-da', 'Jesus'. You can imagine the intense excitement when it became increasingly clear that the children could speak and hear.

Twenty-two youngsters were carefully tested and only two failed the test. We prayed a second time for these. Afterwards I used short sentences and other words that were quickly repeated. Some of the parents were weeping for joy, hugging their children and giving praise and glory to God. Those present will never forget the radiant faces of those West African children whose deaf ears were opened and dumb tongues were loosed by the wonderful Power of God.

Elizabeth Way – crippled with arthritis – divinely healed

(Elizabeth Way's testimony)

'The first sign of arthritis appeared with a swelling in my finger. It spread rapidly to my legs and body, paining me severely. My doctor promptly sent me to hospital where they diagnosed rheumatoid arthritis. Being the mother of four children I dreaded the thought of being confined to a wheelchair.

As my health deteriorated I realised I needed God's help. My husband persuaded me to attend Rev. Peter Scothern's Divine healing service at Bath. I listened to the faith message and went forward to the laying on of hands in Jesus' Name.

After a few ministries I made a remarkable recovery and today I am completely free of every trace of arthritis. I give God all the glory.'

(*Elizabeth Way*, Bath, England)

The wonderful healing of Michael Barnes

Occupying the front cover of one of my *Deliverance* magazines is the photo of nine-year-old Michael Barnes. It was during the Seacroft Crusade in the United Reformed Church that Jesus bestowed upon Michael his special miracle.

Started limping
The first sign Michael detected of his illness was a stiffening of the knee. As this condition intensified he started limping badly. This was followed by a high temperature, which resulted in a visit to the Leeds dispensary. After careful

examination Michael was immediately admitted to the James Hospital. For four weeks he was subjected to observation and tests, and eventually transferred to a children's hospital.

The specialist in charge of this case gave no hope of immediate recovery, and told Mrs Barnes that it would be a prolonged illness. Michael's legs were scheduled to be in plaster for many wearying months.

Receiving this disheartening news Mrs Barnes attended my Deliverance and Healing Crusade. Special prayer was offered for Michael and a handkerchief prayed over in accordance with Acts 19:11–12.

This was taken to the children's hospital, and placed over Michael's legs with the nurses prayerfully co-operating.

Amazing recovery
Within days Michael made a most remarkable recovery. He was soon discharged from the hospital completely cured. Within two weeks he was home again enjoying a normal life. Every trace of osteomyelitis disappeared.

Michael Barnes is now a young man who remains fit and well. He can run and jump without weakness or pain. For many years he has proved the goodness of God.

This young lad was destined to months of suffering but God's power met his great need. What the Lord has wrought in the life of Michael Barnes **He is willing to do for anyone who will trust and obey Him.**

Jesus said,

> *'Suffer the little children to come unto me, and forbid them not: for of such is the Kingdom of God. Verily I say unto you, Whosoever shall not receive the kingdom of God as a little child, he shall not enter therein. And he took them up in his arms, put his hands upon them, and blessed them.'* (Mark 10:14–16)

> **'With men this is impossible; but with God all things are possible.'** (Matthew 19:26)

Peter Scothern would welcome your genuine enquiries and prayer requests. Crusade Schedules are available. Please see the back of this book for contact details.

Chapter 7

Jesus – His Divine Blueprint

I resolutely believe that the book of Acts is the divine blueprint for the Church of today. Christians and churches should now be experiencing the wonders of God's power and glory comparable with that of the first-century Church.

God's message undermined

What scriptural authority have we to 'water down' and 'dilute' the Holy Spirit inspired message and ministry of the book of Acts. Our present dilemma, through unbelief and lack of dedication to New Testament standards has left the Church in a precarious position. No longer does her voice and opinion impact our sin-stricken society.

Modern philosophy proposes that we act **like**

the world to win the world. This fanciful concept may fill our pews with pretenders but not with genuine born-again believers. This philosophy has cost us dear. It has compromised our message and rendered our ministry of little effect.

We must zealously pursue the **Blueprint of the Book of Acts**.

The early Church record

The book of Acts is an inspired record of the deeds and accomplishments of the first-century Church. As today we are so fascinated by statistics and results, let us examine the early Church record.

How about this . . .

1. A company of some one hundred and twenty first-century Christians gathered in the Upper Room, Jerusalem, on the memorable day of Pentecost. Note, not a vast number, just over one hundred. They sought God's promise of the Holy Spirit in persistent prayer and total dedication, experiencing a remarkable unity of purpose and vision. They were all filled and saturated with the mighty power of the Holy Spirit.

God's power thrust them into the streets of the city among the public with a convicting, converting message plus miraculous manifestation.

Result – 3,000 are added to the kingdom of God (see Acts chapter 2).

2. Peter and John journeying to a prayer meeting see a crippled man begging **outside** the temple. They demonstrate God's love and compassion and the crippled man is miraculously healed (see Acts chapter 3).

   Result – A further 5,000 are added to the kingdom of God (Acts 4:4).

3. Evangelist Philip preached the Gospel with signs following in the city of Samaria. The inhabitants responded hearing the message and witnessing the miracles and signs from heaven.

   Result – the city turned to Christ in a mass gospel response (see Acts chapter 8).

4. In the Acts chapter 17 we read of the Gospel with Divine signs and miracles impacting whole communities. Reference is made to Christ's disciples **turning the world upside-down**.

God's way is the best way

Can anyone suggest a more improved, a more successful means of winning the world for Christ?

I repeat the book of Acts is God's blueprint for fruitful evangelism.

I have proved this with fifty-five years of dedicated ministry. West Wales was moved by the power of the gospel in the 1970s when God confirmed His message with miracles of healing and deliverance.

India was stirred by the gospel when I preached there with signs following.

20,000 gathered in Sierra Leone during the 1980s to hear God's message and witness the blind to see, the deaf to hear and the lame to walk in Jesus' Name. Surely God can do it again!

But the modern-day Church must reconsider its man-made traditions; its carnal activities and compromising messages. We must seek after the Holy Spirit's power and return to the methods and ministry of the first-century Church. Some may argue that times have changed. Reader – the basic needs haven't changed. Sin still blights the human race. Folk still die prematurely with disease and sickness. The world is still cursed with demons from the underworld. We must return to a Holy Ghost ministry comparable with the New Testament, book of Acts era. We must open our Bibles and emphatically declare the book of Acts is God's way of reaching our generation for Christ.

Yes, there is a price to pay!

The price we must pay

This price involves:

- an uncompromising obedience to the instructions and directions of the Holy Spirit;

- a complete yielding to the prompting and dictates of the Lord;

- a bold, steadfast declaration of the pure gospel with its compelling acts of obedience, as declared by Peter at Pentecost;

- a convicting call to repentance, to baptism in water and filling with the Holy Ghost.

'Then Peter said unto them, Repent, and be baptised every one of you in the name of Jesus Christ for the remission of sins, and ye shall receive the gift of the Holy Ghost.' (Acts 2:38)

Couple this God-ordained message with divine manifestation and we have a formidable method of winning the world for Christ.

The book of Acts adequately proves this and we should pursue this ideal with zealous dedication. For fifty-five years I have held tenaciously to this belief. What I have experienced and witnessed has proved to me beyond all doubt that the book of Acts is the divine blueprint to turn this present world upside-down for God.

I am praying the Lord will raise up a mighty army of dedicated Christians, born of God's Spirit and filled with His power and glory who will shake this world once again with the glorious gospel of Jesus Christ and mighty signs from heaven.

Chapter 8

Jesus –
Alive Beyond the Veil

The joy of the disconsolate disciples knew no bounds when they discovered Jesus was alive again.

> '[Jesus] *showed unto them his hands and his side. Then were the disciples glad, when they saw the Lord.'*   (John 20:20)

> '[Jesus] *shewed himself alive after his passion* [crucifixion] ***by many infallible proofs,*** *being seen of them* ***forty days,*** *and speaking of things pertaining to the kingdom of God.'*
>   (Acts 1:3, my emphasis)

The vital question

During those remarkable forty days the disciples of Jesus would ask a myriad questions.

Undoubtedly one prevalent question would be: 'What transpired during the three days between Your death on the cross and the resurrection?' The apostle Peter carefully detailed the answer. In his first epistle he records this remarkable statement:

> 'For Christ also hath once suffered for sins, the just for the unjust, that he might bring us to God, being put to death in the flesh, but quickened by the Spirit: by which also he went and preached unto the spirits in prison; which sometime were disobedient, when once the long-suffering of God waited in the days of Noah, while the ark was a preparing, wherein few, that is, eight souls were saved by water.'   (1 Peter 3:18–20)

Clarification is also to be found in Acts 13:35–37:

> 'Wherefore he saith also in another psalm, Thou shalt not suffer thine Holy One to see corruption. For David, after he had served his own generation by the will of God, fell on sleep, and was laid unto his fathers, and saw corruption: but he, whom God raised again, saw no corruption.'

The Psalmist David predicted many accurate aspects of Jesus' life, death and resurrection, which were literally fulfilled.

Jesus also visited **Paradise** after His crucifixion. He promised the dying thief who was crucified with Him:

> *'And he said unto Jesus, Lord, remember me when thou comest into thy kingdom.*
> *And Jesus said unto him, Verily I say unto thee, To day shalt thou be with me in paradise.'*
> (Luke 23:42–43)

An amazing accomplishment

Jesus, having departed from His natural body, visited **Paradise** and **Hades** (**Hell**) according to the Scriptures. His departed spirit retained the ability to speak, for He **preached** to the spirits in prison. Jesus' spirit could also **see and hear** having retained the senses of sight and hearing. So beyond life's veil and this natural realm, Jesus continued to communicate and make His presence known. What an amazing feat! So there is life and existence beyond the veil of death: Jesus proved this beyond a shadow of doubt.

Paul's remarkable encounter

Teenage Paul was a degenerate. He was the black sheep of a family that feared God and lived righteously. Paul's rebel attitude involved drug addiction. Such was his involvement that having failed his drug suppliers, they almost killed him. Paul lay in a **coma in hospital** for many days. I was asked by his despairing relatives to visit and pray for him. When Paul eventually awakened from his coma, his first words were – 'Where is Jesus?' This astonished the nursing staff. Paul so persisted asking for Jesus they thought his mind was affected. When I visited again I discovered that Paul had had an out-of-body experience. He had encountered **Jesus** beyond the veil. Jesus had told Paul that he would not depart this life, but return to witness for Him.

A remarkable transformation

Paul's life was completely turned upside down. Before his tragic trauma he was a young man caught up in the web of evil. But his life was totally transformed. He is now a caring Christian, born-again of the Spirit of God. He simply lives for Jesus and is happily married to a Christian partner – an amazing testimony! Jesus lives beyond the veil and Paul's remarkable experience proves it.

Another similar experience

I have prayed with others who for one reason or another were in a coma. A close friend of mine was visiting a local shopping precinct with his wife. Suddenly he slumped to the floor without warning. Anxious attendants came to the rescue. The paramedics quickly arrived and conveyed him to the local hospital. En route my friend had an out-of-body experience. He seemed to rise away from the ambulance and the world disappeared beneath him. He was engulfed by a brilliant light, which surrounded him. Out of the light stepped **Jesus**. Jesus said to my friend, 'I have allowed this to happen to you to prove that I am alive. You will return to earth and testify accordingly.' My friend is now a dedicated born-again believer and relates his encounter with Jesus to many folk. With firm conviction and assurance he repeatedly tells his wonderful story. I have experienced a variety of similar happenings.

Life after death

Reader, there is life after death. We do exist beyond the veil. I have been privileged to link many uncertain souls with Jesus before departing this life. They have passed on with peace and assurance. I continue to receive ongoing evidence that Jesus is alive beyond the veil but blessed are they that have not seen and yet have believed that Jesus is **the Son of Almighty God**.

Chapter 9

Jesus – God's Incomparable Miracle Worker

Jesus would frequently say, 'If you do not believe My words, My true identity, believe Me for the miracles, signs and wonders I have performed':

> 'If I do not the works of my Father, believe me not. But if I do, though ye believe not me, believe the works: that ye may know, and believe, that the Father is in me, and I in him.'
>
> (John 10:37–38)

Even Nicodemus, entrenched in the Jewish religion, had to admit:

> '... no man can do these miracles that thou doest, except God be with him.'
>
> (John 3:2, my emphasis)

Learned and wise, Nicodemus had sufficient sense and insight to see that Jesus' miracles came from God and not from any other source. No other person in human history had produced such conclusive, irrefutable evidence of his claim to be the Son of God.

Jealous opposition

In fact it was this convincing weight of miraculous evidence that filled the minds of His religious opponents with intense jealousy. Furthermore, the miracles Jesus performed were always for the good and blessing of humanity. Never once during His entire ministry did Jesus work one miracle for personal profit or self-glory.

Reader, can you name any other person throughout human history who has generated the following miracles?

- Jesus opened the eyes of the blind – some completely blind from birth.

- Jesus unstopped the ears of the totally deaf and made the dumb to speak.

- Jesus instantly healed all manner of sickness and disease.

- Jesus cleansed and healed the lepers with a touch of His hands.

- Jesus raised at least three dead folk back to life.

   Lazarus of Bethany was dead four days and laid in the sepulchre when Jesus resurrected him. Lazarus became a bishop of the church in Gaul and lived many years.

Miracles in Galilee

- Jesus fed 5,000 and 4,000 hungry folk with a few small loaves and fishes.

- Jesus walked on the Sea of Galilee and calmed a raging storm with just three words of command – *'Peace, be still.'*

- Jesus turned water into the best wine and astounded the wedding guests in Cana of Galilee.

- Jesus cast out many evil spirits setting the captives free.

   One incident involved a mad man who was possessed with 5,000 demons. Legion of Gadara was completely emancipated.

- Jesus received confirmation from heaven that He pleased God and was the Son of God.

- Jesus restored limbs that were disfigured and deformed.

- Jesus changed and transformed the lives of prostitutes, criminals, fraudsters, and sinners.

- Jesus confronted satan in the wilderness and gloriously triumphed over him.

- Jesus predicted His future with accurate detail.

- Jesus also predicted the total destruction of the City of Jerusalem, which occurred in AD 70.

Jesus promised resurrection

- Jesus foretold of His death by crucifixion.
  This was accurately fulfilled to the letter.

- Jesus promised He would rise again on the third day and kept this promise.
  For forty days He personally proved His resurrection by numerous appearances and infallible evidence.

- Jesus foretold His ascension to heaven from the Mount of Olives and 500 gathered to witness this amazing event.

- Jesus continued to prove He was alive following His ascension by empowering **His Name** to work ongoing miracles.

Jesus **continues** to prove that he is alive **today** by empowering His Name to perform a continuous stream of miracles of grace and healing.

Jesus, the same today!

Again, I affirm that no other person throughout history has produced such infallible proof, such amazing evidence of his true identity as **Jesus, the son of the living God**.

The writer to the Hebrews emphatically declares:

> *'Jesus Christ, the same yesterday, and today, and for ever.'*   (Hebrews 13:8)

In other words, Jesus lives today to perform His ongoing miracles.

Two thousand years have not diminished His compassion or power to assist those who genuinely call upon His Name.

Whatever the problem, Jesus has the answer and the ability to deal with it.

Our responsibility is to surrender our lives to Him by truly repenting of our sin-stained ways and acknowledging Jesus as our personal Saviour and Lord.

Reader, have you opened your heart and life to the living Christ? Jesus, the miracle worker, awaits your sincere commitment and believing prayer.

Chapter 10

Jesus –
His Challenge to You!

Late one night Jesus encountered a respected ruler of the Jews named Nicodemus. During the detailed conversation, Jesus made clear and plain the absolute necessity of the '**second-birth experience**'. I quote from the Authorized Version of the Bible:

> There was a man of the Pharisees, named Nicodemus, a ruler of the Jews: The same came to Jesus by night, and said unto him, Rabbi, we know that thou art a teacher come from God: for no man can do these miracles that thou doest, except God be with him.
>
> Jesus answered and said unto him, Verily, verily, I say unto thee, Except a man be born again, he cannot see the kingdom of God.

Nicodemus saith unto him, How can a man be born when he is old? can he enter the second time into his mother's womb, and be born?

Jesus answered, Verily, verily, I say unto thee, Except a man be born of water, and of the Spirit, he cannot enter into the kingdom of God. That which is born of the flesh is flesh; and that which is born of the Spirit is spirit. Marvel not that I said unto thee, Ye must be born again. The wind bloweth where it listeth, and thou hearest the sound thereof, but canst not tell whence it cometh, and whither it goeth: so is every one that is born of the Spirit.'

(John 3:1–8)

Jesus made absolutely clear that no-one can **see** or **enter** the kingdom of God without being **born again**. Three times Jesus emphasized this vital, fundamental truth.

▶ *Reader, have you been born again?*
You may be a righteous person, a church attending member, or someone in need of moral transformation. Whoever you are, whatever your background, religion or belief – **Jesus graciously but firmly informs you: *'You must be born again to see or enter the kingdom of god!'***

What is the born-again experience?

To be born again is a life-transforming experience that will affect the way you live, think, talk and act.

- The first birth is after the **natural** order.

- The second birth is after the **spiritual** order.

Through the first birth we inherit our natural character and attributes.

Through the second birth we inherit our divinely inspired spiritual character and attributes.

The only way to become a member of the human family is via natural birth.

The only way to become a member of God's family is via a spiritual birth – the second birth.

The **born-again** experience occurs when the spiritual life and nature of Jesus is implanted into our natural beings:

> *'But as many as received him* [Jesus' nature], *to them gave he power to become the sons of God, even to them that believe on his name: which were born, not* [just] *of blood, nor of the will of the flesh, nor of the will of man, but* [conceived and born] *of God.'* (John 1:12–13, my emphasis)

85

The indwelling Christ

The apostle Paul through his inspired epistles repeatedly emphasizes this amazing truth:

> 'Christ **in** you, the hope of glory.'
> (Colossians 1:27, my emphasis)

> 'I am crucified with Christ: nevertheless I live; yet not I, but Christ liveth **in** me: and the life which I now live in the flesh I live by the faith of the Son of God, who loved me, and gave himself for me.'
> (Galatians 2:20, my emphasis)

> 'For it is God which worketh **in** you both to will and to do of his good pleasure.'
> (Philippians 2:13, my emphasis)

The God of creation has a longing desire to indwell our beings, having been excluded since Adam's downfall. This becomes a reality when we bid Him welcome into our lives.

> 'Behold, I stand at the door, and knock: if any man hear my voice, and open the door, I will come in to him, and will sup with him, and he with me.'
> (Revelation 3:20)

The major obstacle to this divine indwelling is our contaminated natures. In the words of the Bible:

> 'Wherefore, as by one man sin entered into the world, and death by sin; and so death passed upon all men, for that all have sinned.'
>
> (Romans 5:12)

> 'For all have sinned, and come short of the glory of God.'
>
> (Romans 3:23)

Therefore it was necessary for Jesus to provide the means whereby our contaminated hearts could be cleansed from sin and become the dwelling place for God's divine presence. The crucifixion of **Jesus** has made this possible, as explained in chapter 4.

The steps to follow

So the first step must be to acknowledge our sins and shortcomings and earnestly request divine forgiveness through the blood of Jesus. God will respond when we are absolutely genuine and sincere.

The second step is to invite the Holy Spirit of God to implant the spiritual nature of Jesus **in**

our beings. In other words, **welcome Christ into our lives**. Consider once again Revelation 3:20:

> *'Behold, I stand at the door, and knock: if any man hear my voice, and open the door, I will come in to him, and will sup with him, and he with me.'*

Jesus is more willing to respond than we are to receive.

The third step is to act upon the instruction revealed in Romans 10:9–10:

> *'That if thou shalt confess with thy mouth the Lord Jesus, and shalt believe in thine heart that God hath raised him from the dead, thou shalt be saved. For with the heart man believeth unto righteousness; and with the mouth confession is made unto salvation.'*

It is initially advisable to confess your commitment to Christ to some other believer. Also, to meet and fellowship with other 'born-again' Christians. Regularly read the Bible and frequently commune with the Lord in prayer.

I would welcome news of your decision to become a 'born-again' disciple of Jesus, so I can assist you further (see page 91).

Contact and Further Information

Further free literature is available to all sincere enquirers. Your request will be treated with strictest confidence. Please write to:

Peter Scothern Ministries
150 Chatsworth Drive
Mansfield
Notts NG18 4QX
England

Website: www.peterscothernministries.com

(No telephone calls please.)